The Very Very Very Very Last Book Ever: Part One

Front cover cartoon by Mike Williams; back
cover cartoon by Albert Rusling

First published 1986

Printed and bound in Great Britain by Mackays of Chatham Ltd,
for Roger Houghton Ltd, in association with J. M. Dent and Sons Ltd,
Aldine House, 33 Welbeck Street,
London W1M 8LX

British Library Cataloguing in Publication Data

Rusling, Albert
The very very very last book ever.
Part 1
1. Nuclear warfare — Caricatures and
cartoons
I. Title II. Williams, Mike
355'.0217'0207 U263

ISBN 1 85203 000 3

The Very Very Very Last Book Ever: Part One

Albert Rusling and Mike Williams

Roger Houghton
London

Imagine for one moment that the unimaginable has happened. The warning bells sound and a nuclear attack is imminent.

How will people spend those last few minutes?

Will there be resignation?

Countless acts of outstanding heroism, or total chaos?

Now at last, the results of a new survey carried out by the authors can be revealed. But you'd better read quickly, you may not have a great deal of time.

20
Minutes

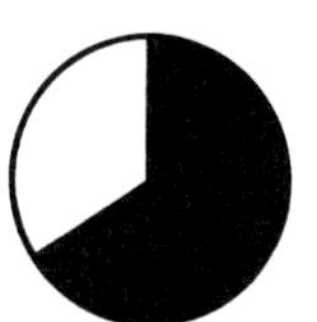

"Thank goodness, I can have a lie in today."

JESUS
SAVES
OFFER ENDS
12-30

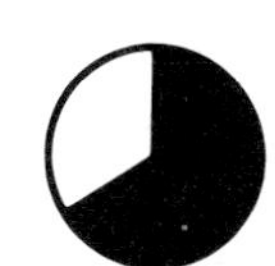

"It's all right, dear, it's an anti-flash cream from Lenthéric."

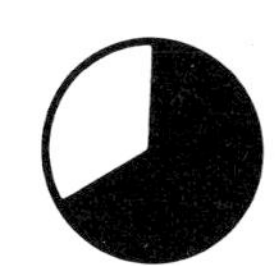

18 HOUR
GIRDLE
REDUCED

*"Oh, mother, I **do** wish I could share Donald's blind faith in the powers of his Swiss army knife."*

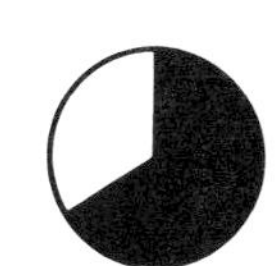

GUINNESS BOOK OF RECORDS

BIGGEST COCK-UP-

STILL AT
PRE NUCLEAR
WINTER
PRICES

KEY'S CUT - WHILE - U - WAIT
USAF

". . . fortunately, I got custody of the elephant."

"Give me an 'M', give me an 'I', give me an 'S', give me an 'S', give me an 'I', give me an 'L', give me . . ."

POST OFFICE
HOLOCAUST COMMEMORATIVES
REPRIEVE

HIGH
NUCLEAR
WINTER
FREEZE

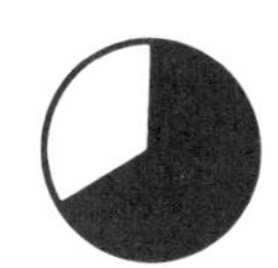

GYPSY ROSE
LAST
EPISODE
DALLAS
£2-50

SPOT THE MISSILE
1ST PRIZE GEIGER COUNTER

"I always said women would get equality one day."

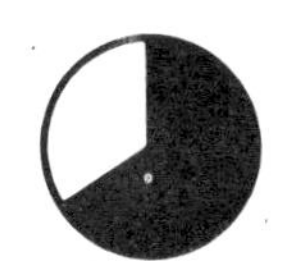

JOKE SHOP
PROTECT AND SURVIVE
H.M. GOVERNMENT

15 Minutes

"O Yes! O Yes! Oh Christ! Oh No! O Yes!"

MINISTER
FOR
ARMAGEDDON
NAMED

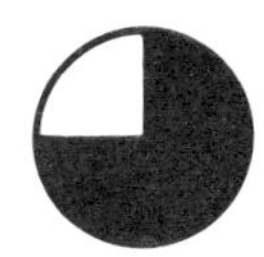

HAD YOUR CHIPS
TAKEAWAY
CLOSED

VASECTOMY
CLINIC
CANCELLATIONS
CANCELLATIONS

"If I've said it once I've said it a thousand times, multilateral disarmament is the only way, and would you listen? . . . And now look what's happened . . . well one thing's for certain, you can't blame this one on me . . . my God if my mother could see me now . . ."

"Looks like we're due for a nuclear strike."

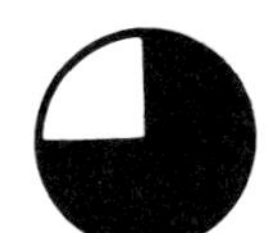

DETERGENT
NEW FORMULA
REMOVES STUBBORN FALLOUT

"Really? Oh thank goodness for that, I was just developing a hell of a stitch."

SAND
SAND
SAND
SAND

USA
I ♥ MY
CRUISE

TIME
AND
MOTION
Dept

"Henry!"

10 Minutes

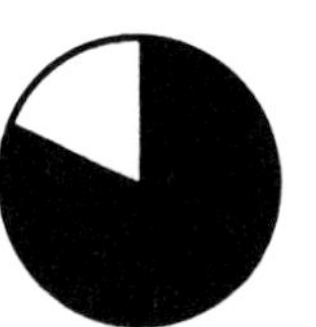

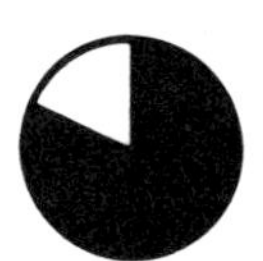

"Men and children first!"

"All the megatons, twenty!"

"Just fink, Sid . . . in the next ten minutes every phone box in the whole world will be vandalised."

"He could have been the best trainer in the business."

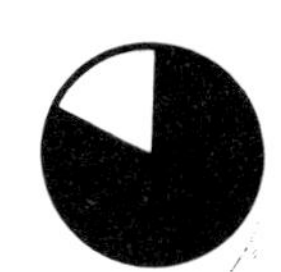

THANK GOODNESS IT'LL BE THE LAST TIME I'LL HAVE TO TALK TO YOU...

VOTE FOR JONES

...PEA BRAINED REMEDIAL MORONS

"Well, let's just hope it's not a false alarm."

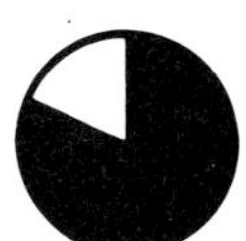

MILLS + BOON
MILLS + BOON
MILLS + BOON
MILLS + BOON
MILLS + BOON
MILLS + BOON

1
2
PAINT
BY
NUMBERS

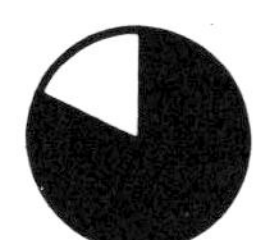

"Ten minutes? Oh dear . . . that it should end this way . . . not on the green, luv . . . we must do something . . ."

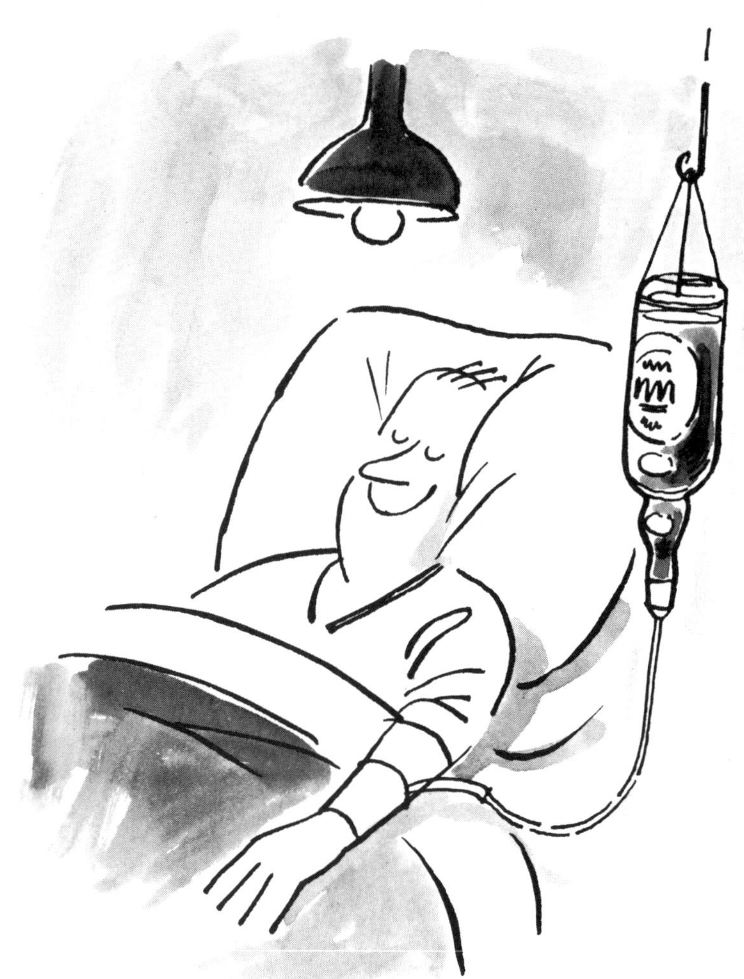

I
ED
NY

"It's the bomb, modom."

4
Minutes

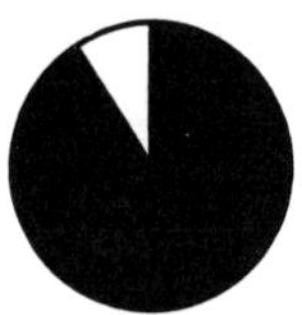

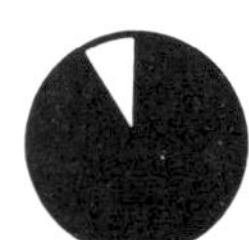

"Well, what should we do for the other two minutes?"

JOKES + NOVELTYS

BARBIE DOLL
FLASH SUIT

"Roughly translated, Chief: white man says welcome Umbuktu to the twentieth century . . . unfortunately his magic word machine has just said, 'Goodnight Vienna, you've got just four minutes to party on down'."

FIVE
GO
LOOTING

"Sorry comrade, this one's taken."

"Don't panic, Simpson, but I think we've run out of egg and cucumber."

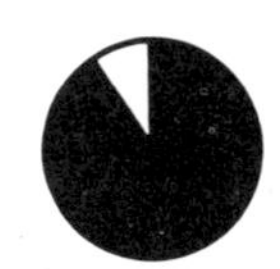

FIRE

FIRE

FIRE

"Four minutes? Damn. Oi'll have to re-set, mine's due to go in eight."

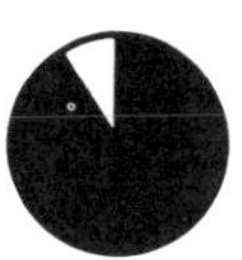

WATCH
TOWER

THERE'S AN OLD MILL
BY THE STREAM NELLIE.....

ALCOHOLICS
ANNON

COUNCIL
SHELTER

"There goes the neighbourhood."

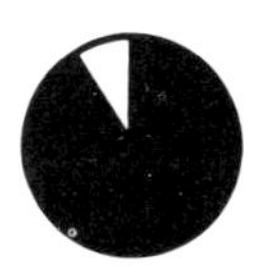

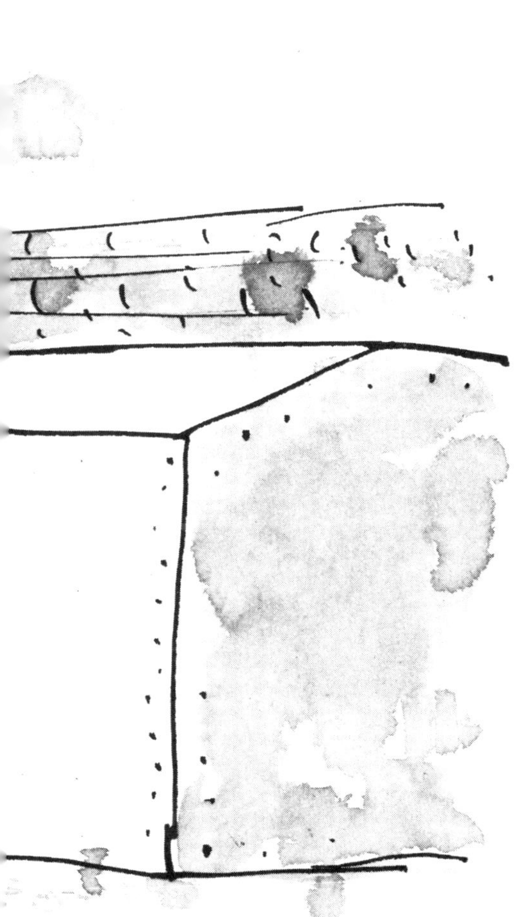

"Reg, is it all right if mother . . .?"

"... And to think they laughed when you declared our garden a nuclear-free zone."

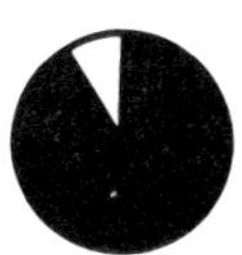

"He didn't see his wife coming."

HOT
LINE

DUNLOP
4
MINS
FERODO
5

2
Minutes

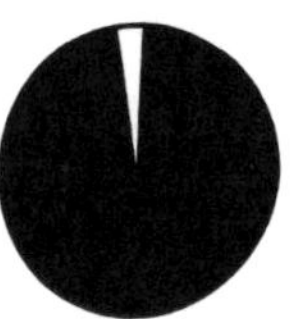

"For what we are about to receive . . ."

SHELTER 7
TUPPERW
TUPPER
TUPPERWARE
TUPPERWARE
TUPPERWARE
TUPPERWARE

LIVERPOOL FOOTBALL CLUB

WAIT
SHELTER

"Bagged two more of the blighters, m'dear."

LEGO

FALLOUT
PAPER
WEIGHTS

MICROWAVE

"For God's sakes, Marjorie, stop worrying!
Mr Gorbachov's already cancelled the milk!"

"I'm sure the shelter's around here, somewhere behind the delphiniums."

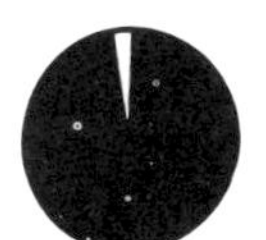

PANIC
A-GRAM
YOU HAVE
TWO
MINUTES

LAST WILL
AND TESTAMEI

CEEFAX
PRAYERS
OSHEA
DEMOLITION.

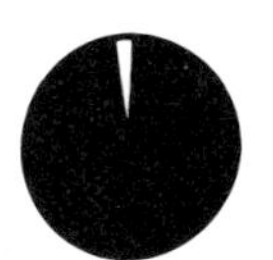

BELLS
AFORE
YE GO

DIAL A
SONG
GOODBYEEE
GOODBYEEE
WE WISH YOU ALL
THE BES......

THRUST INC.
MISSILE DIVISION

"Here we go! Here we go! Here we go!"

BANG!